PRESCHOOLER'S CATHOLIC

BIBLE ACTIVITIES

ASCENSION

Time Period Name	Time Period Color	Book(s) of the Bible
Early World	Turquoise	Genesis 1–11
Patriarchs	Burgundy	Genesis 12–50
Egypt & Exodus	Red	Exodus
Desert Wanderings	Tan	Numbers
Conquest & Judges	Green	Joshua; Judges; 1 Samuel 1–8
Royal Kingdom	Purple	1 Samuel 9–31; 2 Samuel; 1 Kings 1–11
Divided Kingdom	Black	1 Kings 12–22; 2 Kings 1–16
Exile	Baby Blue	2 Kings 17–25
Return	Yellow	Ezra; Nehemiah
Maccabean Revolt	Orange	1 Maccabees
Messianic Fulfillment	Gold	Luke
The Church	White	Acts

All *Great Adventure Kids* books are color-coded to show where each story fits in Bible history. This makes it easy to discover how the people and events of the Bible fit together to reveal the remarkable story of our Faith. For more information, visit **ascensionpress.com**.

Originally published as *Preschoolers Best Activity Bible* by Scandinavia Publishing (Copenhagen).

This edition published 2020 by Ascension Publishing Group, LLC. Editorial review by Amy Welborn.

Copyright © 2019 Scandinavia Publishing House

Drejervej 15, DK-2400 Copenhagen, NV, Denmark E-mail: info@sph.as, www.sph.as Designed by Scandinavia Publishing House Illustrator: Sandrine L'Amour Text: Andrew Newton Activities, layout, and cover: Gao Hanyu Activity Editor: Linda Vium

Unless otherwise noted, Bible verses are from the *Revised Standard Version Bible, Second Catholic Edition*. Copyright © 2006 Division of Christian Education of the National Council of the Churches of Christ in the United States of America.

Ascension PO Box 1990 West Chester, PA 19380 1-800-376-0520

ISBN 978-1-950784-25-7

Contents

The Garden of Eden

Genesis 1–3

In the beginning, God made everything. He created the world and all the plants and animals that live in it. He even made the first people, Adam and Eve. God said that the world he had made was very good, and he planted a beautiful garden for Adam and Eve to live in with him. Unfortunately, Adam and Eve soon sinned, which meant they had to leave the garden that God had made for them.

FIND THE SHADOW

Draw a line to the right shadow for each animal.

COUNT THE ANIMALS GOD CREATED

Write the correct number in each box.

Butterfly [ ]   Bee [ ]

Parrot [ ]   Fox [ ]

FIND THE FIRST LETTER FOR EACH WORD

Draw a line from the letter to the right word.

F   _IRAFFE   

T   _ONKEY

G   _ION

L   _LOWER

M   _REE   

COLOR THE BIBLE VERSE

I AM WONDROUSLY MADE.

PSALM 139:14

COUNTING GAME

Add up the animals and write down the number for each line.

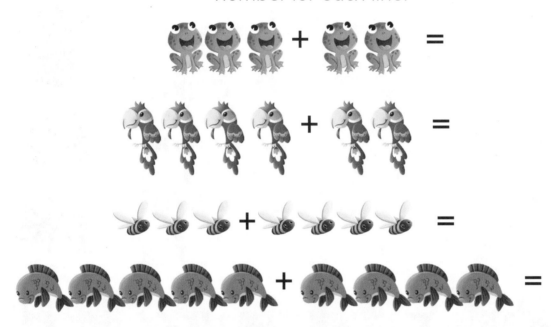

SPOT THE ODD ONE

Circle the parrot that is different from the others.

SPOT THE DIFFERENCES

Find the 7 differences between these two pictures.

Saved from the Flood

Genesis 6–8

"Noah, build an ark," God said. "The world has become so evil that I must wipe it out and start over." Noah built the ark, and God sent him two of every kind of animal. Soon a flood covered the whole world, but God kept Noah, his family, and the animals safe on the ark.

WORD SEARCH

Find the words in the word search puzzle.

ARK

TREE

BIRD

A	N	B	I	R	D
S	O	N	X	T	A
L	A	D	D	E	R
S	H	A	O	G	K
Q	H	B	G	U	C
L	T	R	E	E	M

DOG

LADDER

SON   NOAH

FIND THE PAIR

Circle the 2 pictures of Noah's son that are exactly the same.

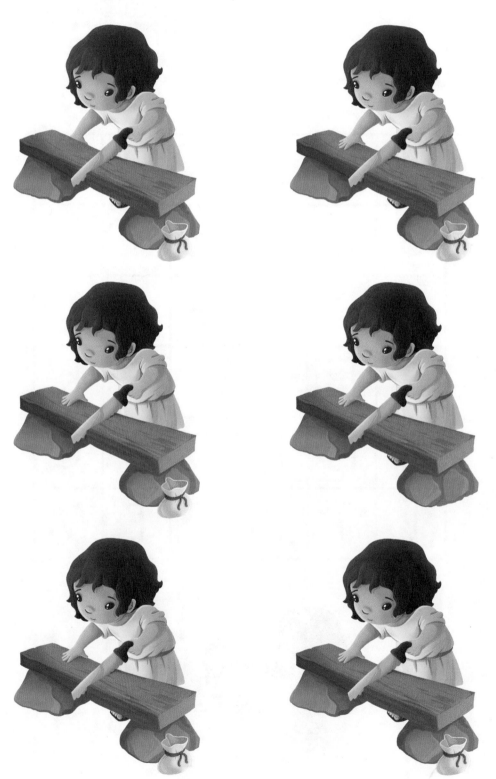

FIND THE OBJECTS

Circle the objects and animals in the picture below.

 BIRD
 **RABBIT**
 SNAIL
 **AX**
 SACK

 **LADDER**
 **BAG**
 **HAMMER**
 HEDGEHOG
 SAW

FIND THE RIGHT WAY

Help the lions find the ark.

DOT TO DOT

Connect the dots to see where the animals went.

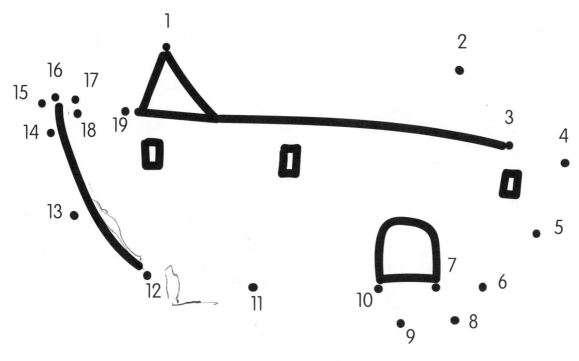

COLOR THE RAINBOW

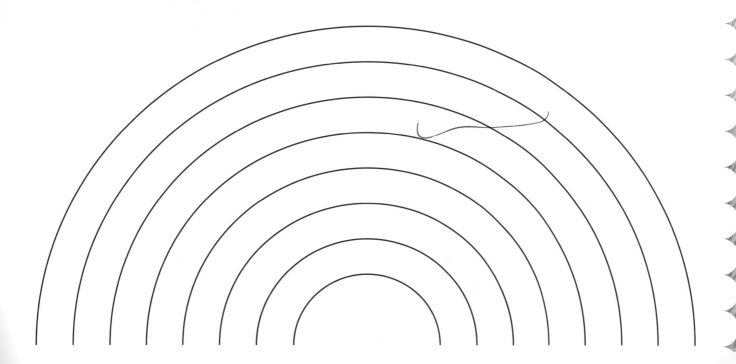

God Keeps His Promise

Genesis 12:1-9; 21:1-7

"Abraham," God said, "I will bless you and make your family into a great nation." Abraham loved God and believed him, but Abraham was old and didn't have any children. God can do anything, and he kept his promise. Abraham and his wife Sarah had a baby boy named Isaac, even though they were old.

COUNT THE LETTERS IN THE WORDS

Count the letters and write the number in the box.

ABRAHAM   CAMEL   TENT   DESERT   FRIEND

THE BIGGEST AND SMALLEST

Circle the biggest and the smallest camel.

FOR I KNOW THE PLANS I HAVE FOR YOU

JEREMIAH 29:11

SPOT THE DIFFERENCES

Find the 7 differences between these two pictures.

FIND THE RIGHT WAY

Help Isaac find his way to his parents.

STICKER GAME

Find stickers for the missing pieces on page 114 and complete the picture.

Joseph Forgives His Brothers

Genesis 37; 39–45

Joseph's brothers were jealous of him, so they sold him as a slave. God took care of Joseph and used him to help Egypt prepare for a famine. When Joseph's brothers came to buy food, who sold it to them? It was Joseph! "I forgive you," he said. "You wanted to hurt me, but God used it for good."

FOLLOW THE LETTERS

Follow each letter and write it down in the square at the bottom. You will find a word from the story.

R T E B S O H R

□ □ □ □ □ □ □ □

WORD SEARCH

Find the words in the word search puzzle.

FATHER

COAT

ANGRY

S	L	A	V	E	F
Y	P	E	D	G	A
A	N	G	R	Y	T
J	O	S	E	P	H
L	C	O	A	T	E
A	R	H	M	N	R

SLAVE

EGYPT

JOSEPH

FIND THE PAIR

Circle the 2 pictures that are exactly the same.

FIND THE SHADOW

Circle the shadow that belongs to Joseph.

SHAPE PUZZLE

Complete the scene with the shape stickers on page 115.

The Escape Through the Sea

Exodus 1–14

Moses' mother put him in a floating basket to protect him from the king who wanted to kill all the baby boys. The princess of Egypt found him and raised him as her son. Later, God sent Moses to set his people free. God parted the water of the sea so they could escape the king's army.

SPOT THE ODD ONE

Circle the picture that is different from the others.

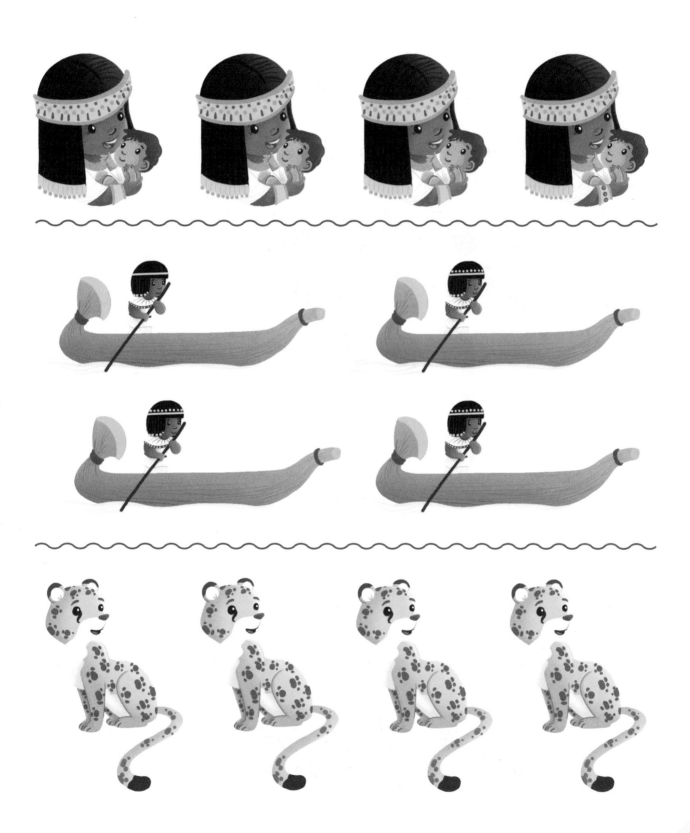

MATCH BY COUNT

Count how many animals are in each box and draw a line to the right number.

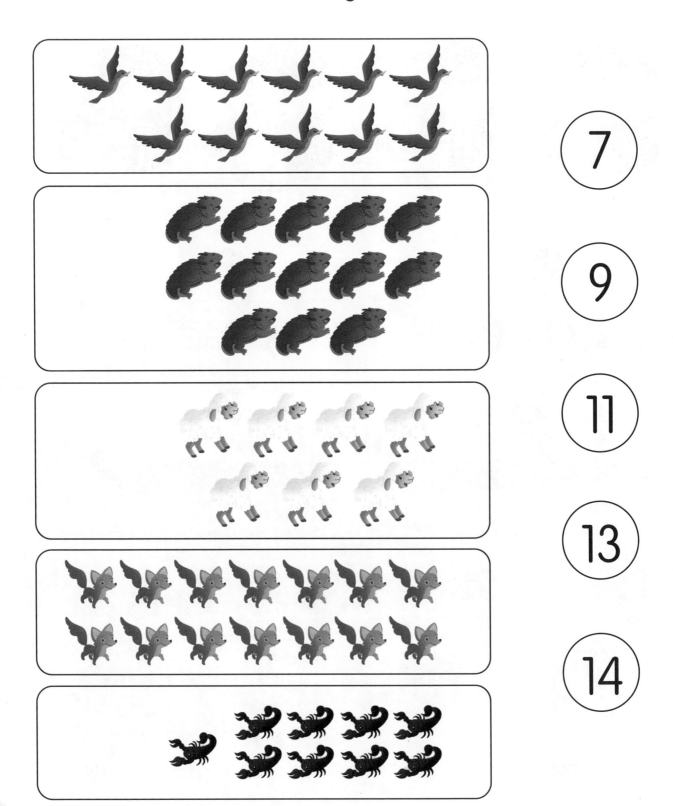

SPOT THE DIFFERENCES

Find the 7 differences between these two pictures.

LET MY PEOPLE GO.

EXODUS 8:1

LINK THE FIRST LETTER IN EACH WORD

Draw a line from the letter to the right word.

S   _RINCESS

O   _OSES

P   _HEEP

E   _CTOPUS

M   _GYPT

32

FIND THE RIGHT WAY

Help the people find their way to Moses.

A New Family for Ruth and Naomi

The Book of Ruth

Ruth was Naomi's daughter-in-law. They were all alone because they had both lost their husbands. Ruth took care of Naomi and gathered food for them in a field. The man who owned the field was Naomi's relative, Boaz. Boaz and Ruth got married and had a baby boy. Now Ruth and Naomi had a new family!

COUNT THE LETTERS

Count the letters and write the number in the box.

NAOMI   HUSBAND   BOAZ   FAMILY   RELATIVE

DOT TO DOT

Connect the dots to see what animal it is.

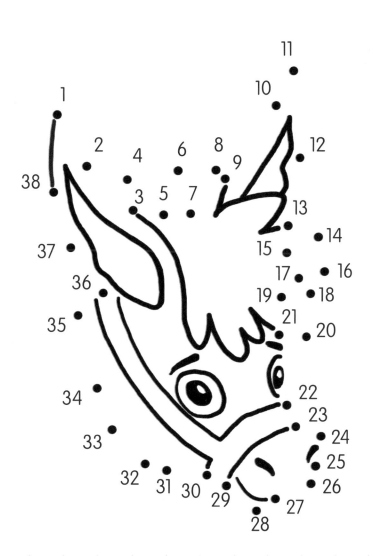

FIND THE PAIR

Circle the 2 pictures that are exactly the same.

SPOT THE DIFFERENCES

Find the 7 differences between these two pictures.

FIND THE RIGHT WAY

Help Boaz find the way to Ruth.

FIND THE SHADOW

Circle the shadow that belongs to Ruth.

David Trusts in God

1 Samuel 17

David was a shepherd boy. One day, he was bringing food to his brothers in the army. Everyone in the army was afraid of a giant enemy warrior named Goliath. David said, "I will fight Goliath." All David had was a sling and some stones, but he trusted God. Goliath went down in one hit!

COUNTING GAME

Add up the animals and write down the number for each line.

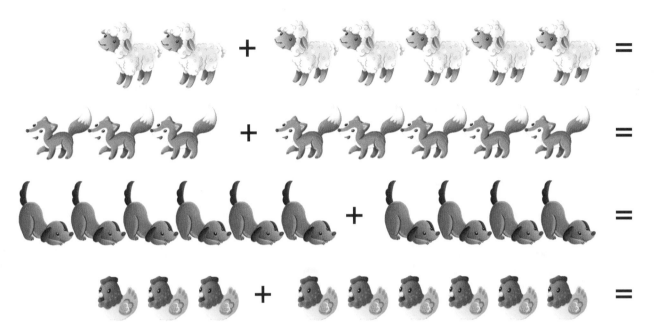

COLOR THE BIBLE VERSE

The Lord is with me; I am not afraid.

PSALM 118:6 (NAB)

WORD SEARCH

Find the words in the word search puzzle.

SWORD

DAVID

S	L	D	V	E	F
W	P	A	R	M	Y
O	N	V	R	Y	T
R	O	I	E	P	H
D	A	D	X	D	E
A	R	F	E	A	R

DAD

FEAR

ARMY

SHAPE PUZZLE

Complete the scene with the shape stickers on page 115.

SPOT THE ODD ONE

Circle the picture that is different from the others.

STICKER GAME

Find stickers for the missing pieces on page 114 and complete the picture.

Fire from Heaven

1 Kings 18:20-39

Elijah was sad that so many people worshiped idols instead of God. He challenged the idol worshipers to a contest. "Whoever's God sends fire on their altar is the one true God," he said.

The idol worshipers prayed and prayed, but nothing happened. Elijah prayed, and fire covered the whole altar, even though it was soaking wet!

COUNT THE PEOPLE

How many children do you see in the picture on the left?

How many people are wearing head coverings?

How many people are there altogether?

WRITE THE WORDS

Look at the words and try to write them below.

ELIJAH

FIRE

PEOPLE

_____   _____   _____

THE BIGGEST AND SMALLEST

Circle the biggest and the smallest dog.

COLOR BY NUMBER

Color the picture below using the color code.

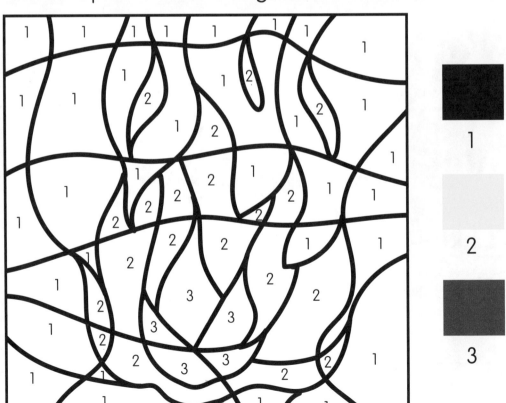

1

2

3

SPOT THE DIFFERENCES

Find the 7 differences between these two pictures.

WHO IS NOT IN THE PICTURE?

Circle the person who is not in this picture.

FIND THE PAIR

Circle the 2 pictures that are exactly the same.

Jonah Runs from God

The Book of Jonah

God told Jonah to go to Nineveh, but he didn't want to. Instead, he ran away on a boat. A huge storm scared the sailors. "It's my fault. Throw me overboard," Jonah said. A big whale came and swallowed Jonah. After three days, it spit him out on the shore. Then Jonah obeyed God and went straight to Nineveh.

Find the words in the word search puzzle.

JONAH

CRAB

CAT

Q	B	Z	C	R	K
J	O	N	A	H	A
L	A	D	T	L	R
S	T	R	E	E	K
W	H	A	L	E	C
L	C	R	A	B	X

TREE

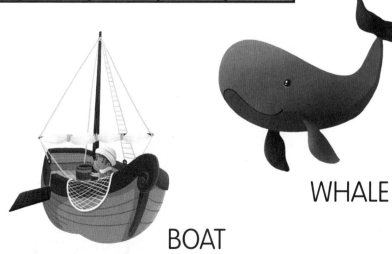

BOAT

WHALE

COUNTING GAME

Add up the animals and write down the number for each line.

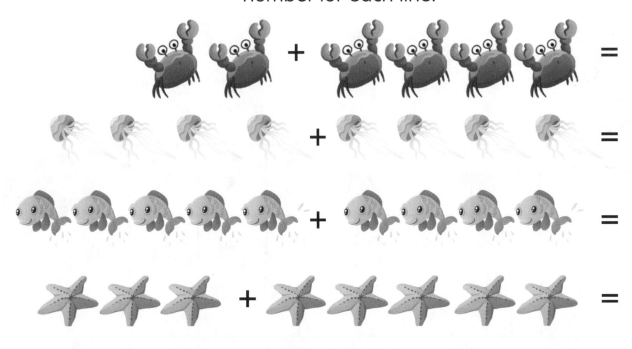

COLOR THE BIBLE VERSE

Trust in the Lord with all your heart.

PROVERBS 3:5

FIND THE RIGHT WAY

Help Jonah find the boat.

Connect the dots to see what animal it is.

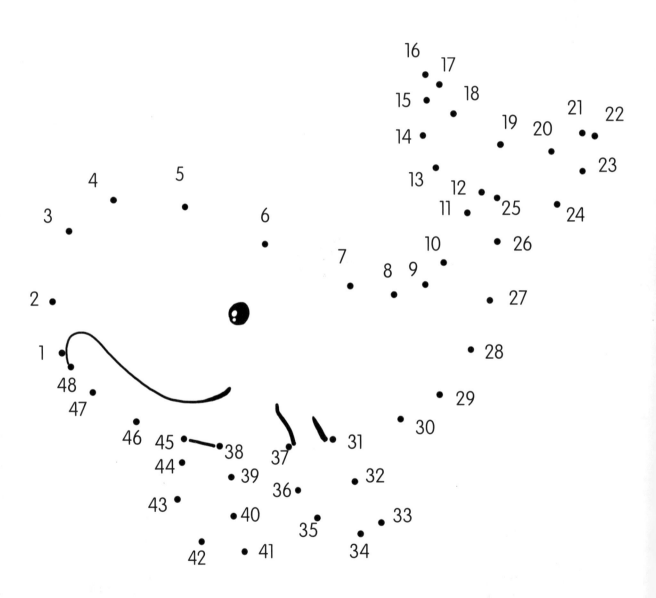

FOLLOW THE LETTERS

Follow each letter and write it down in the square at the bottom. You will find a word from the story.

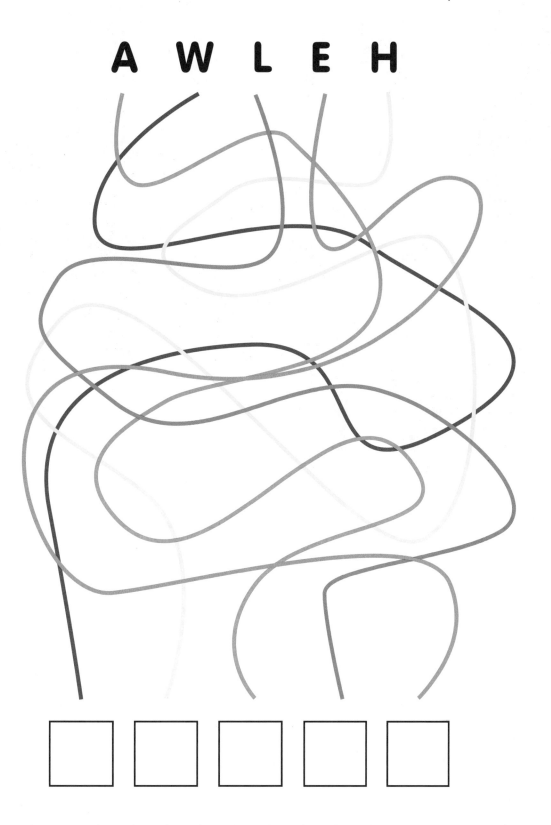

A   W   L   E   H

The Birth of Jesus

Matthew 2:1-12; Luke 2:1-20

Mary was about to have a baby. This wasn't just any baby. It was God's own Son. Mary and her husband Joseph went to Bethlehem. Angels told nearby shepherds the good news. A bright star shone overhead and led some wise men from far away to come worship baby Jesus, too. They brought gifts of gold and rare spices for the newborn King.

SPOT THE ODD ONE

Circle the picture that is different from the others.

FOR TO US A CHILD IS BORN, TO US A SON IS GIVEN.

ISAIAH 9:6

WRITE THE WORDS

Look at the words and try to write them below.

DONKEY   JESUS   STAR

_____ _____ _____

FIND THE SHADOW

Circle the shadow that belongs to the picture.

FIND THE RIGHT WAY

Help the wise men find baby Jesus

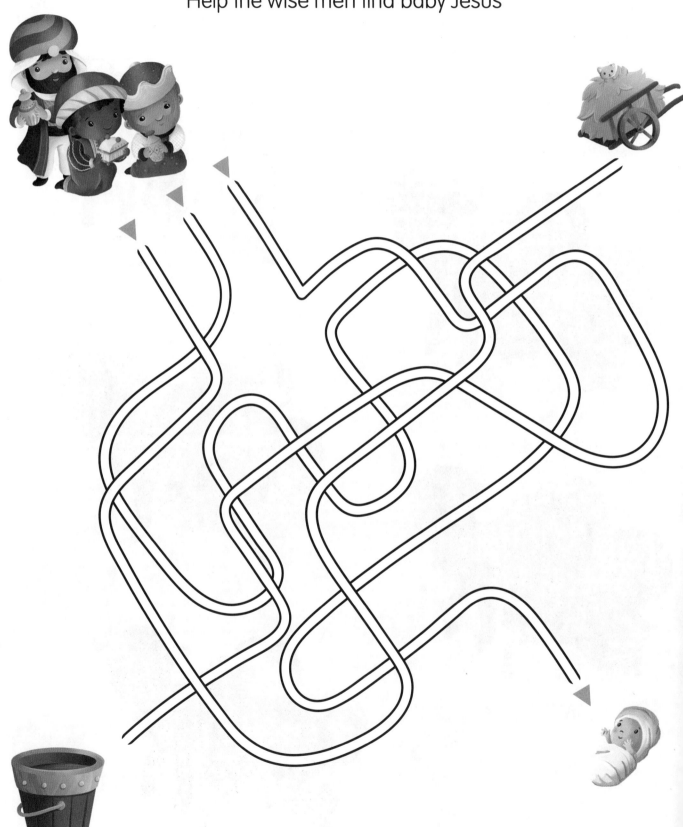

SPOT AND COUNT

How many people are there in this picture? ☐

How many animals do you see? ☐

How many gifts can you find? ☐

Jesus Calls His Disciples

Matthew 4:18-22; Luke 6:12-16

When Jesus was all grown up, he called twelve men to be his close friends, his disciples. He taught these men, and they followed him wherever he went. Some of them used to be fishermen, and some used to be tax collectors, but now they all followed Jesus and told others about him.

COUNT THE LETTERS IN THE NAMES

Count the letters and write the number in the box.

JESUS   JOHN   MATTHEW   ANDREW   BARTHOLOMEW

☐   ☐   ☐   ☐   ☐

SPOT THE ODD ONE

Circle the picture that is different from the others.

SHAPE PUZZLE

Complete the scene with the
shape stickers on page 115.

SPOT THE DIFFERENCES

Find the 7 differences between these two pictures.

FIND THE RIGHT WAY

Help the disciple find Jesus.

WHO IS LEFT?

Cross out all the people that appear twice in the grid.
Who is left?

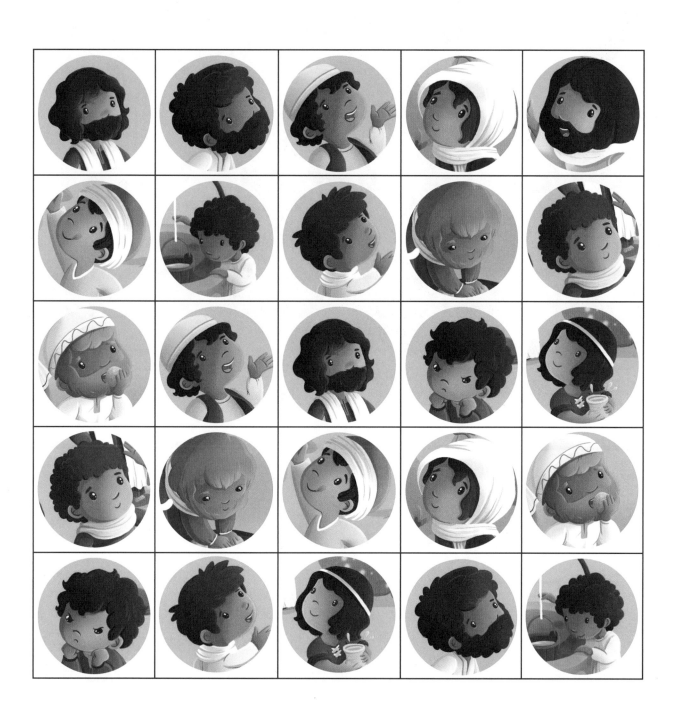

Jesus Calms the Storm

Mark 4:35-41

Jesus and his disciples were crossing the sea when a big storm blew up and almost sank their boat. "Jesus, wake up!" the disciples cried. "We're going to drown!" Jesus stood up and said, "Wind, waves, stop it!" The storm stopped right away, and all the disciples were amazed.

WORD SEARCH

Find the words in the word search puzzle.

JESUS

PETER

MOON

M	J	E	S	U	S
O	S	N	P	H	A
O	A	D	E	F	I
N	T	R	T	I	L
W	A	V	E	S	M
L	C	R	R	H	T

WAVES

SAIL

FISH

FIND THE OBJECTS

Circle the objects and animals in the picture below.

 BARREL

 **BIRD**

 FISH

 **SQUID**

 ROPE

 MOUSE

 HEAD COVERING

 CAT

 MOON

 PADDLE

DOT TO DOT

Connect the dots to see what animal it is.

LINK THE FIRST LETTER IN EACH WORD

Draw a line from the letter to the right word.

S		_IRD
B		_OPE
S		_TAR
R		_ADDLE
P		_QUID

Circle the 2 pictures that are exactly the same.

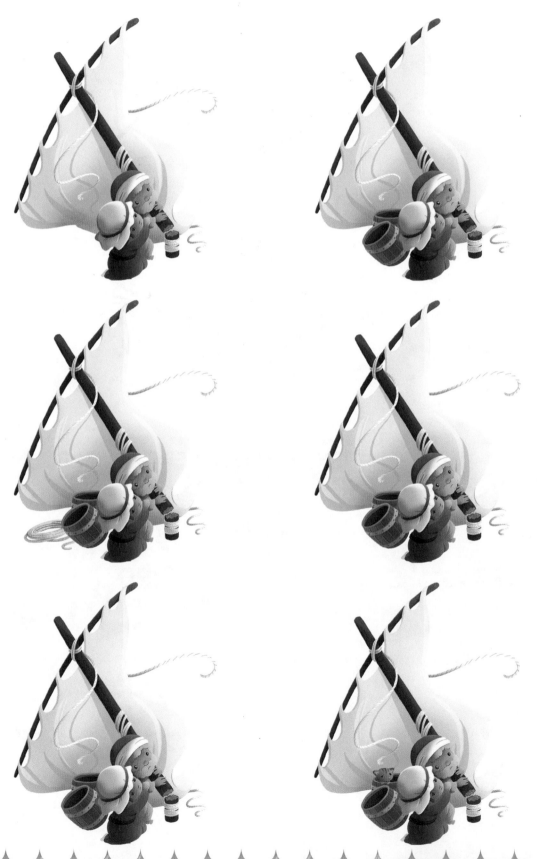

Follow each letter and write it down in the square at the bottom. You will find a word from the story.

M   T   S   O   R

Jesus Heals a Little Girl

Mark 5:21-43

A man named Jairus came to ask Jesus to heal his daughter. When they were on their way, a servant came and told him that she was dead. "Don't be afraid," Jesus said. "Just believe." Jesus took the dead girl's hand and said, "Little girl, get up." Just like that, she was alive and well!

COLOR THE BIBLE VERSE

FOR WITH GOD NOTHING WILL BE IMPOSSIBLE.

LUKE 1:37

SPOT THE ODD ONE

Circle the picture that is different from the others.

SHAPE PUZZLE

Complete the scene with the
shape stickers on page 115.

SPOT THE DIFFERENCES

Find the 7 differences between these two pictures.

FIND THE RIGHT WAY

Help Jairus come to Jesus.

FIND THE SHADOW

Circle the shadow that belongs to the picture.

Jesus Welcomes the Children

Matthew 19:13-14

Some parents wanted to bring their children to see Jesus. The disciples thought he was too busy and important to bother with them. Jesus scolded them and said, "Let the little children come to me, and do not stop them. The kingdom of God belongs to those who have faith like a child."

WORD SEARCH

Find the words in the word search puzzle.

GIRL

BOY

FROG

F	R	O	G	U	S
I	S	N	I	H	A
O	U	D	R	F	M
N	N	B	L	I	O
W	D	O	G	Z	M
L	C	Y	R	W	T

DOG

SUN

MOM

LET THE CHILDREN COME TO ME.

MATTHEW 19:14

THE BIGGEST AND SMALLEST

Circle the biggest and the smallest dog.

STICKER GAME

Find stickers for the missing pieces on page 114 and complete the picture.

SPOT THE ODD ONES

Circle the things that are not supposed to be in the picture.

SPOT AND COUNT

How many men have beards?

How many shoes can you see in the picture?

How many children can you see?

How many people are wearing green clothes?

Zacchaeus Meets Jesus

Luke 19:1-10

Zacchaeus didn't have many friends because he was a tax collector. He was short, so he had to climb a tree to see Jesus over the crowd. When Jesus saw him, he said, "Come down from there. I want to go to your house today!" Zacchaeus was so happy that Jesus wanted to be his friend! He ran home and prepared a feast for his new friend, and promised that he would help the people he had hurt before.

FIND THE SHADOW

Draw a line to the right shadow for each person.

COUNTING GAME

Add up the food and write down the number for each line.

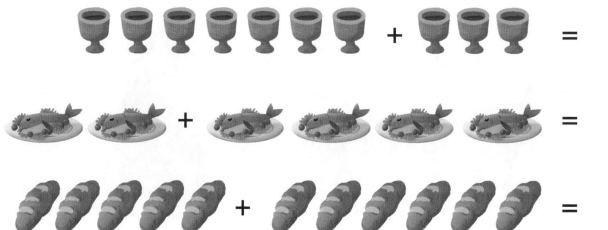

COLOR BY NUMBER

Color the picture below using the color code.

FIND THE RIGHT WAY

Help Zacchaeus find Jesus.

SHAPE PUZZLE

Complete the scene with the
shape stickers on page 115.

SPOT THE DIFFERENCES

Find the 7 differences between these two pictures.

Jesus Enters Jerusalem

Mark 11:1-11

Jesus and his disciples were on their way to Jerusalem for an important festival. He sent them to find a donkey that he could ride on, and they found it just where he said. On the way into the city, people laid down their jackets and waved palm branches, welcoming him and praising God. "Hosanna!" the people sang.

WRITE THE FIRST LETTER

Look at the pictures, and write the first letter of the word.

_alm

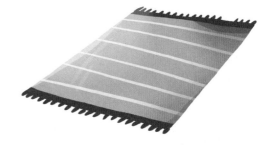

_ug

_acket

_onkey

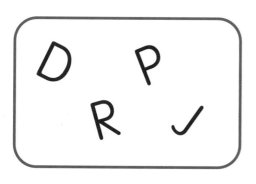

D P
R ✓

SPOT THE ODD ONE

Circle the picture that is different from the others.

STICKER GAME

Find stickers for the missing pieces on page 114 and complete the picture.

FIND THE OBJECTS

Circle the objects and animals in the picture below.

 PALM

 JAR

 MOUSE

 ORANGES

 RUG

 CAT

 DONKEY

 PALM TREES

 JACKET

DOT TO DOT

Connect the dots to see what it is.

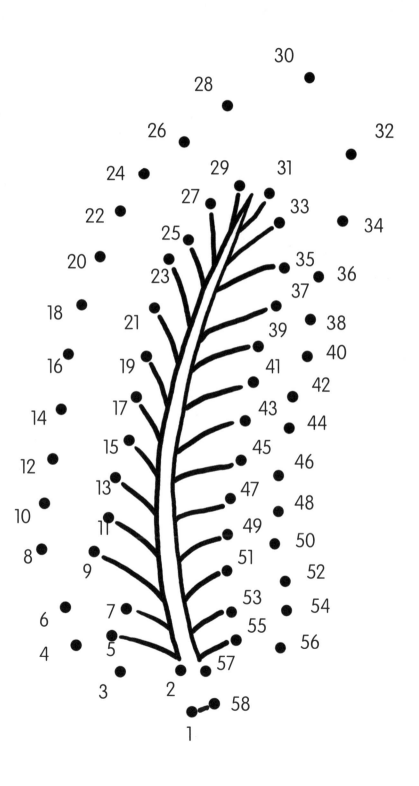

Jesus Dies and Rises Again

Matthew 27:11–28:10

The leaders of Jerusalem put Jesus to death even though he had never done anything wrong. Jesus let them do this because he wanted to pay the price for all of our sins. After the disciples buried him, Jesus rose again! An angel told Mary Magdalene and another Mary, "He is not here. He has risen!"

WORD SEARCH

Find the words in the word search puzzle.

JESUS

TOMB

CROSS

F	Z	T	G	U	S
C	R	O	S	S	A
O	I	M	R	F	V
N	S	B	L	I	I
J	E	S	U	S	O
L	N	Y	R	W	R

RISEN

SAVIOR

FOLLOW THE LETTERS

Follow each letter and write it down in the square at the bottom. You will find a word from the story.

R   E   N   S   I

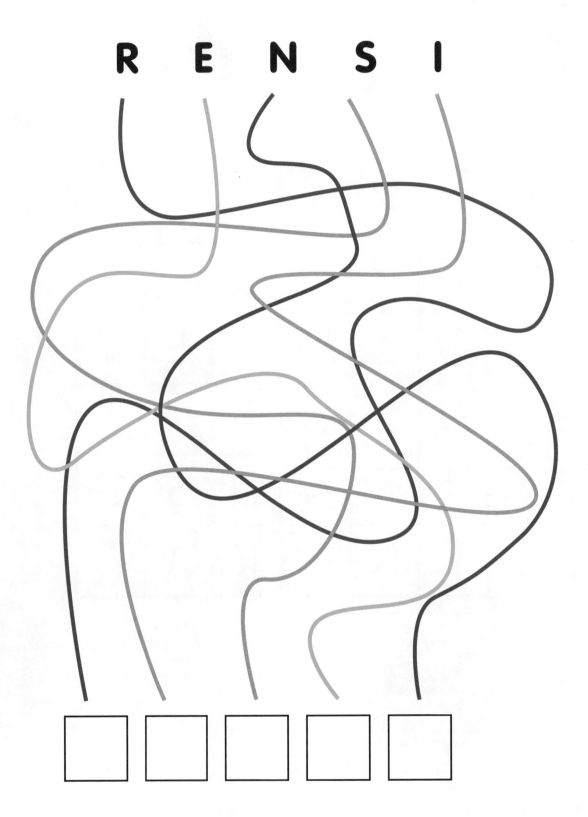

☐ ☐ ☐ ☐ ☐

FIND THE PAIR

Circle the 2 pictures that are exactly the same.

SPOT THE DIFFERENCES

Find the 7 differences between these two pictures.

HE IS NOT HERE, BUT HAS RISEN!

LUKE 24:5

GAME SOLUTIONS

Page 5

Page 6

Butterfly	3	Bee	9
Bird	2	Fox	1

Page 7

F ─────── _IRAFFE
T ─────── _ONKEY
G ─────── _ION
L ─────── _LOWER
M ─────── _REE

Page 8

Page 9

Page 11

A	N	B	I	R	D
S	O	N	X	T	A
L	A	D	D	E	R
S	H	A	O	G	K
Q	H	B	G	U	C
L	T	R	E	E	M

Page 13

Page 14

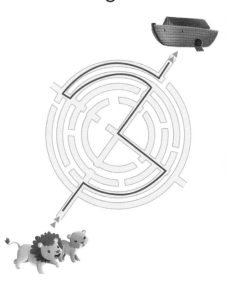

Page 17

7	5	4	6	6

Page 8

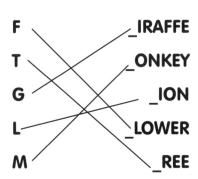

🐸🐸🐸 + 🐸🐸 = **5**

🦜🦜🦜🦜 + 🦜🦜 = **6**

🐝🐝🐝 + 🐝🐝🐝🐝 = **7**

 +  = **9**

Page 12

Page 17

GAME SOLUTIONS

Page 19

Page 25

Page 31

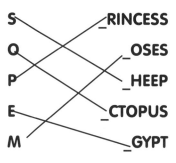

Page 20

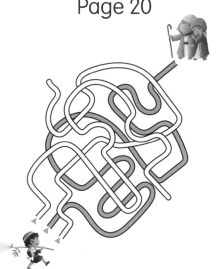

Page 26

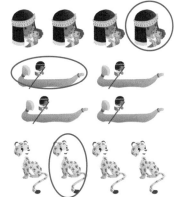

Page 32

S   _RINCESS

Q   _OSES

P   _HEEP

E   _CTOPUS

M   _GYPT

Page 33

Page 23

BROTHERS

Page 29

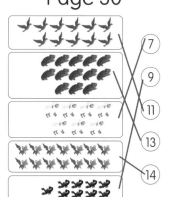

Page 24

S	L	A	V	E	F
Y	P	E	D	G	A
A	N	G	R	Y	T
J	O	S	E	P	H
L	C	O	A	T	E
A	R	H	M	N	R

Page 30

7
9
11
13
14

Page 35

5	7	4	6	8

GAME SOLUTIONS

Page 36

Page 37

Page 38

Page 39

Page 41

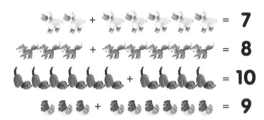

= 7

= 8

= 10

= 9

Page 42

S	L	D	V	E	F
W	P	A	R	M	Y
O	N	V	R	Y	T
R	O	I	E	P	H
D	A	D	X	D	E
A	R	F	E	A	R

Page 44

Page 47

4

5

10

Page 48

Page 49

Page 50

Page 51

GAME SOLUTIONS

Page 53

Q	B	Z	C	R	K
J	O	N	A	H	A
L	A	D	T	L	R
S	T	R	E	E	K
W	H	A	L	E	C
L	C	R	A	B	X

Page 54

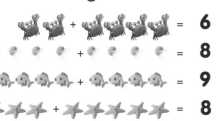 = **6**

= **8**

= **9**

= **8**

Page 55

Page 57

WHALE

Page 59

Page 61

Page 62

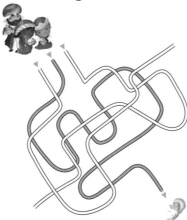

Page 63

6

9

3

Page 65

5   4   7   6   11

Page 65

Page 67

Page 68

GAME SOLUTIONS

Page 69

Page 71

M	J	E	S	U	S
O	S	N	P	H	A
O	A	D	E	F	I
N	T	R	T	I	L
W	A	V	E	S	M
L	C	R	R	H	T

Page 72

Page 73

S   _IRD

B   _OPE

S   _TAR

R   _ADDLE

P   _QUID

Page 74

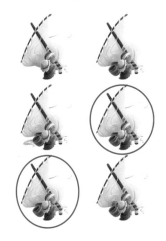

Page 75

STORM

Page 77

Page 79

Page 80

Page 81

Page 83

F	R	O	G	U	S
I	S	N	I	H	A
O	U	D	R	F	M
N	N	B	L	I	O
W	D	O	G	Z	M
L	C	Y	R	W	T

Page 84

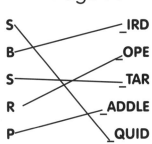

GAME SOLUTIONS

Page 86

Page 87

3
20
8
5

Page 89

Page 90

🍷🍷🍷🍷🍷 + 🍷🍷🍷 = **10**

🐟 + 🐟🐟🐟🐟🐟 = **6**

🍞🍞 + 🍞🍞🍞🍞🍞🍞🍞🍞🍞 = **11**

Page 91

Page 93

Page 95

Palm   Rug

Jacket   Donkey

Page 96

Page 98

Page 101

F	Z	T	G	U	S	S
C	R	O	S	S		A
O	I	M	R	F		V
N	S	B	L	I		I
J	E	S	U	S		O
L	N	Y	R	W		R

Page 102

RISEN

Page 103

Page 104